The Romans

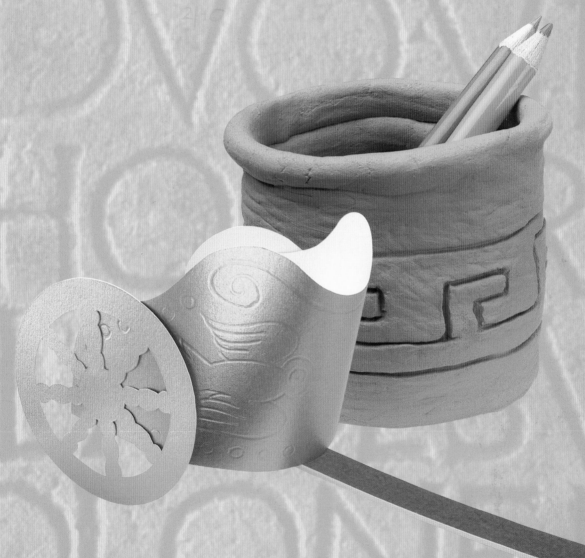

Written by Sally Hewitt

W
FRANKLIN WATTS
LONDON·SYDNEY

This edition 2010

First published in 2006 by Franklin Watts
338 Euston Road, London NW1 3BH

Franklin Watts Australia
Hachette Children's Books
Level 17/207 Kent Street, Sydney NSW 2000

Editor: Rachel Tonkin
Designers: Rachel Hamdi and Holly Fulbrook
Picture researcher: Diana Morris
Craft models made by: Anna-Marie D'Cruz
Map artwork: Ian Thompson

Picture credits:
Bibliothèque des Arts Decoratifs, Paris, France/Bridgeman Art
Library: 26t; The British Museum/HIP/Topfoto: 8bl, 10tr, 18bl,
23t; Werner Forman Archive: 14, 17t, 24t, 24b; HIP/Topfoto: 9t,
20bl, 20tr, 21tr, 26t; Gilles Mermet/AKG Images: front cover t;
Museum of London/HIP/Topfoto: 10bl, 22t;
Picturepoint/Topfoto: 7t, 8r; R. Sheridan/Ancient Art &
Architecture Collection: 6, 12, 15t, 18tr, 22b, 25t; Watts
Publishing: front cover b, 17b; S. Williams/Ancient Art &
Architecture Collection: 16.

All other images: Steve Shott

With thanks to our models: Taylor Fulton and Ammar Duffus

Every attempt has been made to clear copyright.
Should there be any inadvertent omission please
apply to the publisher for rectification.

A CIP catalogue record for this book
is available from the British Library

ISBN: 978 0 7496 9653 5

Dewey Classification: 937

Printed in China

Contents

The Romans

The Romans were the people of the city of Rome. They built a powerful **empire** that lasted for nearly 500 years from 27 BCE to 476 CE. According to **legend**, Rome was built in 753 BCE by twin brothers Romulus and Remus who were brought up by a mother wolf.

This statue shows the twins with the wolf. Rome was named after Romulus.

Rome

The city of Rome became very powerful with grand government buildings, temples, bath houses, theatres and statues. The remains of the buildings of ancient Rome can still be seen today. Today, Rome is the capital city of Italy.

Roads, bridges and ships

The Romans were clever **engineers**. They built thousands of kilometers of roads with bridges over rivers and valleys, and ships that sailed the Mediterranean Sea. Roads and ships allowed the Romans to travel quickly and **conquer** surrounding countries.

Empire

At the height of its power, the Roman Empire spread across North Africa right through Europe to far away Britain.

The Colosseum, where Romans watched **gladiators** fight, still stands in Rome today.

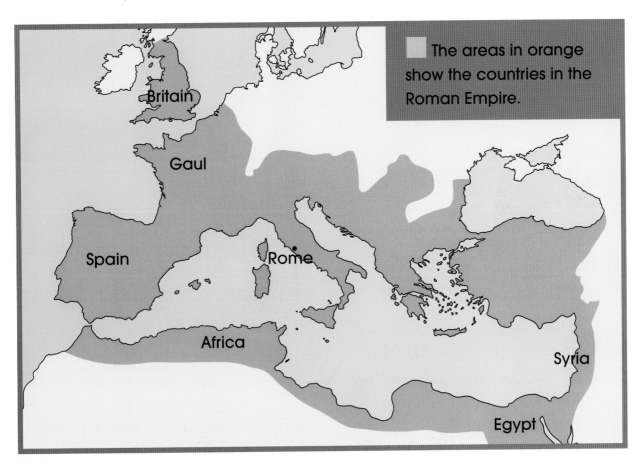

The areas in orange show the countries in the Roman Empire.

Britain

Gaul

Spain

Rome

Africa

Syria

Egypt

Roman emperors

At first, Rome was ruled by kings and then by an elected **senate**. However, as the city's power grew, **senators** and army generals fought to control Roman lands. Eventually one person took over, the emperor.

The first emperor

Many people thought the famous Roman general, Julius Caesar, would be the first Roman Emperor. But he was murdered. A few years later in 27 BCE, his nephew, Augustus Caesar, became the first of 49 emperors.

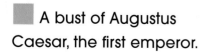

A bust of Augustus Caesar, the first emperor.

The senators of Rome wore **togas** and leather sandals.

Emperor god

Roman emperors were very powerful. The emperor's head was stamped on Roman coins. Emperors were worshipped like gods. Temples were built to them all over the Empire.

The head of the Emperor was stamped on Roman coins.

Make a laurel wreath

Emperors were not kings and they did not wear crowns. They wore wreaths made from laurel to celebrate victory and power.

▶ 1 Cut out a band of dark green card about 4 cm wide to fit around your head.

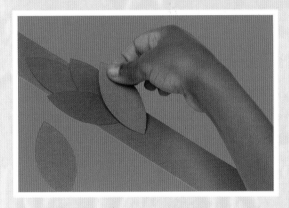

▶ 3 Glue the ends of the band together. Put on your wreath and become a Roman emperor.

▶ 2 Cut out about 20 leaf shapes from more green card. Stick the leaves onto the band so that they overlap.

The army

The Roman army was very successful. The soldiers were well trained. Their job was to **conquer** and control the lands they invaded. The army was important to the Emperor and he made sure his soldiers were looked after.

A soldier wore sandals with leather straps for marching.

Soldier

A soldier joined the army for 25 years. He was paid in money and in salt. His weapons were a stabbing sword and a spear, and he was protected by a helmet, body armour and a large rectangular shield.

Marching

During a war, soldiers marched up to 32 kilometres a day carrying heavy equipment. They built roads and bridges as they went. Each night, they set up camp and took it down the next day.

Armour was made from metal strips which let soldiers move easily.

Legion

A legion was made up of about 5,000 soldiers called legionaries. They were organised into smaller groups of about 100 soldiers called centuries. A century was led by an officer called a centurion.

Each legion carried a silver eagle **standard** which was the symbol of its power. If the standard was captured by the enemy, the legion broke up.

Make an eagle standard

▶ 1 Copy the shapes below onto card. You will need three of the circle shape. Make the eagle as big as this page.

▶ 2 Using two tubes from rolls of wrapping paper, squash the end of one inside the other.

▶ 3 Paint the shapes and tubes with silver paint.

▶ 4 Stick the painted shapes onto the pole with the eagle at the top.

▶ 5 Decorate with red ribbons to complete the standard.

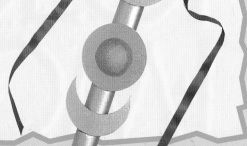

Life in Roman times

Everyone had their place in Roman times. **Citizens** were men who had been born in Rome or had served Rome in a war. Non-citizens were born outside Rome. **Slaves** had no rights and belonged to their owner.

This Roman carving shows mother, father and son. The boy is dressed like his father.

Families

The father was the head of a Roman family. He was expected to look after his wife and children, and their slaves. Families sometimes took in and looked after someone who had no family.

Women

Girls were expected to grow up to be wives and mothers. The women managed the household and the family money.

Slaves

Slaves were either born as slaves or were captives of war. They worked hard as household slaves or on farms or building sites. They were not paid for their work.

Slaves could be badly treated, but sometimes they were treated as members of the family.

Jobs to do

Fetching water

Cleaning

Shopping

Tending the fire

Cooking

Serving at table

Helping the women to dress and do their hair

Looking after the children

Day as a slave

Imagine you are a slave boy or girl in Roman times.

Who owns you? How do they treat you?

Write about a day in the life of a slave boy or girl.

Draw a picture of yourself at work.

Today, important guests are coming to dinner. I'll be in trouble if anything goes wrong!

Houses

A Roman country house was called a **villa**. A town house was called a **domus**. In crowded towns, people lived in apartment blocks four or five stories high, called **insulae**.

Plants and water in the courtyard of this villa helped to keep it cool and shady.

Town house

A town house was built round a central courtyard with a pool for collecting rainwater. The family lived in one part of the house and their slaves in another.

Villa

Remains of Roman villas have been found all over the Roman Empire. They belonged to rich farmers and landowners. They had many rooms which were richly decorated with wall paintings and statues.

Some villas had mosaics, pictures and patterns made of small pieces of stone or tiles. The pictures often told stories of gods and goddesses.

This is a mosaic of Medusa. She had snakes for hair. In myth, anyone who looked at her turned to stone.

Make a Roman mosaic

▶ 1 Copy this outline of a Roman mosaic.

▶ 2 Cut out squares from different coloured pieces of paper.

▶ 3 Paint one section at a time with glue.

▶ 4 Fill each section with coloured squares.

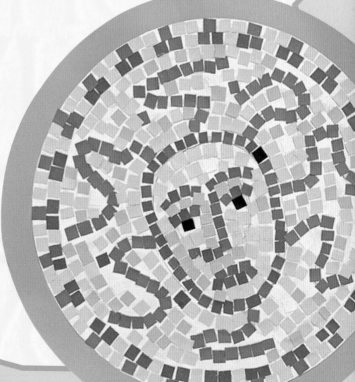

Childhood

The children of slaves and poor people did not go to school. They had to work as soon as they were big enough. In richer families, boys went to school or were taught at home. Girls were sometimes taught to read and write.

Babies

When a new baby was born, it was put at its father's feet. If he accepted the baby, it became part of the family.

Toys and games

Children played marbles and **knuckle bones**, which was a game like modern jacks, and board games. They had dolls and toy animals, flew kites and played on swings and see-saws.

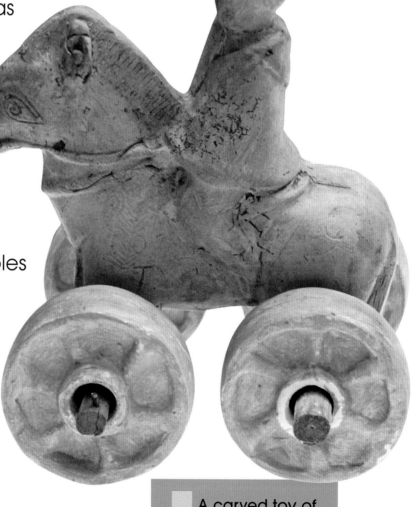

A carved toy of a boy on a horse.

Growing up

Children dressed like their parents and learned to be like them. Boys became adults at 14 and girls when they married aged 13 or 14.

Often, children were given a charm to protect them called a bulla which they kept in a bag hung round their necks.

A Roman boy with a bulla around his neck.

Make a bulla

▶ **1** Think of something that is special to you which will be your secret charm.

▶ **2** Make a model of it in modelling clay and leave it to dry.

▶ **3** Put your charm in a small square of cloth.

▶ **4** Tie the ends of the square with coloured string and hang it round your neck.

Letters and numbers

Latin was spoken in ancient Rome. We call Latin a dead language because nobody speaks it today. Many modern languages, including English, are written in the same alphabet the Romans used.

Roman numerals

Roman **numerals** were 7 letters.

I	V	X	L	C	D	M
1	5	10	50	100	500	1000

MDLXXVI is the year 1576 in Roman numerals (1000 + 500 + 50 +10 + 10 + 5 + 1).

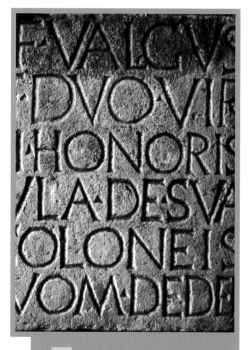

Choose the font TIMES NEW ROMAN on a computer and type some words in capital letters. Compare them to this Roman inscription.

A Roman ink pot, pens and pieces of a writing tablet.

Scrolls

The Romans wrote on rolls of **papyrus** called scrolls with pen and ink.

Children practised writing on wax tablets. They scored letters and numbers with a pointed stylus. The wax could be scraped off to use again.

Make a wax tablet

▶ **1** Rub the end of a candle all over a piece of black card to make a layer of wax.

▶ **2** Cut out a frame of brown card and stick it onto the black card.

▶ **4** When the wax is covered in writing, smooth it with a piece of card.

▶ **5** Rub on a new layer of wax and use the tablet again.

▶ **3** Score Roman letters and numerals into the wax.

Entertainment

The Romans celebrated many religious festivals with entertainments. There were three main kinds of entertainment: plays, games and races. These were each held in a specially designed building.

A Roman mosaic of tragedy (left) and comedy masks.

Theatre

Roman theatres could hold thousands of people. Actors were popular stars, just like they are today. They wore masks so they could be seen from the back seats. The plays were comedies to make people laugh or serious tragedies.

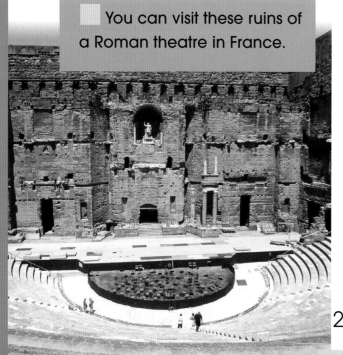

You can visit these ruins of a Roman theatre in France.

Games

Roman games were bloody and deadly. They were held in huge **amphitheatres**, like the Colosseum (see page 7), where crowds gathered to watch gladiator fights and re-enactments of wars. Gladiators were criminals, war captives or slaves. Some were professional fighters.

20

Chariot races

Chariot races were held in the circus or **hippodrome**. Chariots pulled by two or four horses raced around a track. Teams of racers had their own supporters, like football teams have today.

250,000 people could fit into the Circus in Rome to cheer on their team.

Make a model chariot

▶ 1 Copy the shapes below onto gold card and cut out. Score a pattern onto the side with a modelling tool.

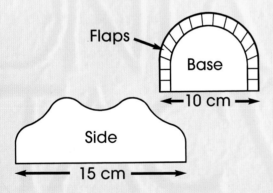

Flaps

Base

←— 10 cm —→

Side

←— 15 cm —→

▶ 2 Snip round the edge of the base and fold up the flaps. Bend the side round the base and glue it on to the flaps.

▶ 3 Cut out two card circles 8 cm wide for the wheels and a T-shape for the chariot pole.

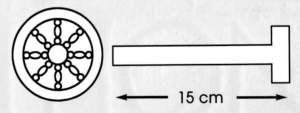

←— 15 cm —→

▶ 4 Either cut out spokes and hub shapes or draw them on. Stick a wheel on each side of the chariot and the T-shape onto the bottom.

Baths

Public baths were places where people met and relaxed. They had central heating and five different kinds of pools. It only cost a penny to get in.

An oil flask and a curved strigil.

Different rooms

The Laconium was a hot room like a sauna with a tub of boiling water.

The Caldarium was a hot room with a hot pool.

The Tepidarium was a warm room with a warm pool.

The Frigidarium had a large, cold pool.

The Spa had mineral water to bathe in and drink for good health.

Washing

Instead of soap, oil was rubbed onto the skin then scraped off with **strigils** which were bone or metal scrapers.

Water in the baths was heated by fires which sent hot air under the floor.

Beauty treatments

Massage, hairdressing, shaving and other beauty treatments were offered at the baths. Slaves helped their masters and mistresses to dress and undress. The clothes were wrapped and held together with belts and pins.

A Roman brooch with a gold coin and a circle of leaves.

Make a dolphin brooch

Dolphin shapes were often used in Roman jewellery.

▶ **1** Cut out the shape of a dolphin in thick card.

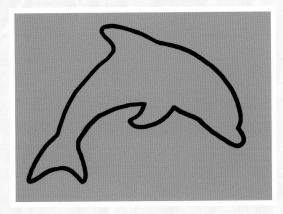

▶ **2** Decorate with shapes of coloured shiny card. Outline the shapes with a silver pen.

▶ **3** Tape a safety pin on the back and pin onto your clothes.

23

Roman towns

In 79 CE, the volcano Vesuvius in Italy erupted and buried the nearby town of Pompeii in ash. The city remained captured in a moment in time under the ash for 1, 600 years until it was rediscovered. The remains show us what a Roman town was like.

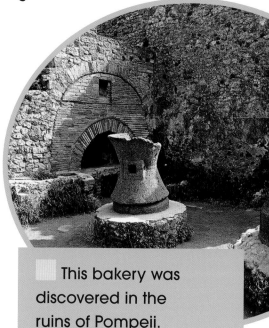

This bakery was discovered in the ruins of Pompeii.

Layout

A typical roman town had two main roads running from north to south and from east to west, meeting at a square in the town centre. Straight streets were lined with gutters which ran into underground sewers. **Aqueducts** carried fresh water into the towns.

Buildings

Throughout the Empire, Roman towns were surrounded by walls. They had temples, bath houses, theatres and an amphitheatre.

You can see the typical straight streets in the ruins of Pompeii.

Shiny red Samian pottery was made in factories and used all over the Empire.

Running a town

Local government was run from a town hall and justice was carried out in the law court. The **forum** was the busy market surrounded by shops, snack bars and inns.

Pottery

In the market you could buy large pottery jars called amphorae which were used for storing food, and also bowls and plates.

Make a simple coil pot

▶ 1 Roll out lots of long sausages of modelling clay.

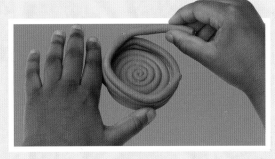

▶ 3 Build up the pot with coils of clay, damping with water as you go to stick the layers of clay together.

▶ 4 Smooth the sides with a modelling tool and mark on a pattern. Leave to dry.

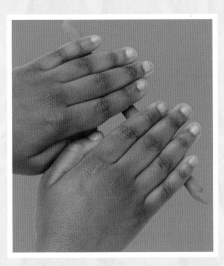

▶ 2 Coil one sausage round to make a flat circle for the base. Damp round the edge with water.

Gods and myths

The Romans worshipped many gods and goddesses. They believed the gods protected the Roman Empire. Towards the end of the Roman Empire, Christianity became the official religion.

This temple in Lebanon was dedicated to the god of wine, Bacchus.

Sacrifice

People brought animals to the temples for **sacrifice** to please the gods. Priests killed the animals on an **altar** and special requests to the gods were made.

Gods and goddesses

Each god or goddess had a role –

Jupiter, king of the gods, was the god of thunder and lightning. He carried a lightning bolt.

Ceres, goddess of the harvest, carried ears of corn.

Diana, goddess of the moon and hunting, carried a bow and arrow.

Mars, the god of war, was said to be the father of Romulus and Remus.

The gods belonged to a family. Stories about them, called myths, explained what happened in the world.

Neptune was the god of the sea and earthquakes. He rode a horse in the waves.

Neptune carried a large three-pronged spear called a trident.

Make a collage of a god or goddess

Chose a Roman god or goddess. Imagine what they would look like. This is Neptune.

▶ Draw them carrying their symbol.

▶ Use pieces of material, coloured paper and wool to give them clothes and hairstyles in the Roman style.

Glossary

Altar

A table on which sacrifices to the gods were made.

Amphitheatre

A round- or oval-shaped building where Roman crowds watched gladiator fights.

Aqueduct

A bridge that carries water.

Citizen

Roman citizens were men who were born in Rome, or who had fought for Rome. People in conquered lands could also become citizens.

Conquer

To attack a place and take control over it. Romans conquered many countries which then became part of the Roman Empire.

Domus

A Roman town house.

Empire

A group of countries ruled by an emperor or empress.

Engineer

A person who designs and builds roads and bridges.

Forum

A public square or marketplace.

Gladiator

A professional fighter who entertained Roman crowds.

Hippodrome

An oval-shaped racing track for horse and chariot racing.

Insulae

A Roman apartment block.

Knuckle bones

A game like modern jacks played with the small bones of animals in Roman times.

Legend

A traditional story that has been passed down through the ages.

Numeral

A symbol that stands for a number.

Papyrus

A kind of paper made from reeds.

Sacrifice

An offering to the gods. Romans brought gifts of food or animals to the temple to be killed to please the gods.

Senate

A group of people who form part of the government.

Senator

A member of a government who has been voted in by the people.

Slave

Slaves were owned by their masters and were not paid for their work.

Standard

A pole carried by a soldier which had the symbol of his legion on it.

Strigil

An instrument used by the Romans for scraping the skin after a bath.

Toga

A loose piece of clothing worn by men in ancient Rome.

Villa

A Roman country house.

Index